FATHER GIVES AND TAKES AWAY
THE JOURNEY HOME

AND GOD WILL WIPE AWAY EVERY
TEAR FROM THEIR EYES; THERE SHALL BE
NO MORE DEATH, NOR SORROW, NOR CRY-
ING. THERE SHALL BE NO MORE PAIN, FOR
THE FORMER THINGS HAVE PASSED AWAY.

REVELATION 21:4

BY JEAN STEPHENS

TRILOGY

Manufactured in the United States of America
10 9 8 7 6 5 4 3 2 1
Library of Congress Cataloging-in-Publication Data is available.
ISBN: 978-1-68556-641-8
E-ISBN: 978-1-68556-642-5

Table of Contents

Dedication

This book is dedicated to Brandon Keith Fuller (my son).

I never dreamed I'd be a mother with a dead son, but here I am to tell you my story of healing and how Jesus turned it all around for me. This was a pain I thought would never go away, but my God came right into this place of grief and mourning and healed it!

You see, I was a naïve twenty-year-old girl that was newly married, expecting the birth of our first child. Everything was complicated from the beginning. This was an indication of how things would turn out. The beginning of the end started with placenta previa and ended with my son coming several weeks early. The doctor told me the baby was in grave danger and may not survive.

I went into delivery to give birth to my son; I was experiencing a lot of hemorrhaging, and I was very afraid, nervous, and anxious. I went through the delivery, but instead of hearing a crying baby, I heard nothing but silence. Then I heard the doctor say, "He is alive!" I remember questioning in my head, *He is alive?* But then I heard scurrying around, trying to handle the baby and me...then complete silence! The nurse looked at me and said, "I'm sorry, he was just too small." What do you mean? What's going on? The baby did not make it? Instead of bringing home a healthy baby boy, I brought nothing but emptiness and sadness to a nursery filled with Winnie the Pooh, but not one sound of my baby.

Immediately we were tasked with making funeral arrangements and decisions, which left me empty and confused. I remember the tiny blue casket and the rainy day, trying to go home after leaving the graveside to a house full of blue flowers and people all around me. I just wanted to wake up, and this would all be a bad dream, but it wasn't! I lay in silence, just wondering where was Jesus and why did this have to happen to me?

Many years later, after four wonderful sons, Jesus showed up for me, and I now realize, He didn't take my baby from me, but He chose me to be an Angel Mom! What an honor that our precious Savior would reach down and choose me to be His vessel for this assignment. I know my precious son was too beautiful for this earth and my Jesus needed and loved him more than I ever could. You see, your kingdom's purpose is always in your deepest pain.

Angels In Waiting 91:4 was birthed out of my deepest pain. I pray many women will find healing through this ministry because giving a baby back to Jesus is always so hard to do, but we must trust Him through the process of healing! Keep your eyes on Jesus and not on your situation. As I stood by that tiny grave, I knew my son was not there but in the arms of Jesus! At the time, all I felt was pain. But now I know it will be a glorious day when I get to see Jesus face to face and meet my son Brandon Keith Fuller for the very first time!

Foreword

I am thrilled and excited to introduce you to my wife, Jean Stephens! When she asked me to write this foreword, I jumped at the opportunity. As an introvert, I don't get terribly excited about a lot of things. But Jean is the highlight of my life, next to my relationship with Jesus Christ, of course.

Jean is easily the godliest woman I have ever had the pleasure of knowing. And I have been fortunate to be related to some true powerhouse women of God. My mom and my grandmothers included. I have never known anyone else with such a deep love and commitment to living a true biblical life.

Jean is a true type-A personality. She is bold and audacious without being offensive most of the time. That being said, she will not hesitate to set you straight, even if it means hurting your feelings a little. She hears the voice of God and is obedient to almost everything He tells her to do, including writing this book. Honestly, she was a little intimidated by it all. But I believed in her from the start.

She is a truly amazing woman of God that is dedicated to living a biblical lifestyle. I have had the pleasure of calling her my wife for the last eleven-plus years. She is easily the best thing that has ever happened to me. She has high expectations of those she loves but also corrects and disciplines in the most loving way possible. I have grown to be a better man, husband, and father mostly because of what God has done through her.

Her discernment and ability to deliver a message are second to none. Because she has experienced the loss of babies in her own life, she is an excellent resource for any of you mothers (and fathers) who have experienced the loss of a life before it even had a chance to start. Most mothers and fathers that have lost a child often suffer in silence. This is where people like Jean can help. Jean knows the pain you are feeling and has an uncanny ability to counsel these families…she doesn't counsel from a professional perspective but from one who has firsthand knowledge of the same pain you are experiencing. She can truly identify with your loss. Be silent no longer; tell your story just like Jean. The enemy wants you to suffer alone, but there is power in the testimony. Go to the Angels In Waiting 91:4 website at www.angelsinwaiting914.com to read many testimonies similar to your story and Jean's story too. While you're at the website, be sure to sign up for the monthly newsletter, where you can receive some biblical nuggets and learn the behind-the-scenes story of Angels In Waiting 91:4.

I know Jean desires healing for you, and through much prayer, her heart for you is a deep and true healing of the emotional, physical and spiritual wounds that you have encountered. Jean is the very definition of an "overcomer." So, this book is a story of hope as much as it is about how the ministry of Angels In Waiting 91:4 was created.

Her story is much, much deeper than what you see here in the pages to follow. Maybe someday soon, you will hear the rest of the story. Her life is truly what best sellers and movies are made of. Enjoy the rest of this book and take heart in knowing that there is hope for healing and life after loss.

Acknowledgments

I would like to thank my husband for walking this journey with me. We have seen the hand of God on our family, over and over! We are blessed and highly favored by the King.

I would also like to thank my sons, daughters-in-law, and grandchildren for every little thing you have done to support me and to help this ministry thrive.

Also, to all the ladies who volunteer each week at Angels In Waiting 91:4, without your dedication, love, and support, this ministry could not run. You have all shown yourselves worthy of the calling He has placed on each of us. We give Him all the thanks and praise!

I would especially like to thank my primary mentor, a woman's pastor who guides select mentees. This godly woman has been critical to my spiritual growth and is a valuable part of my life. She is my spiritual mama, and I love her dearly. I have learned much about biblical Hebrew, which has brought a whole new meaning to the biblical text. She is my "Elijah," and I dread the day when she is no longer part of my life.

I also wanted to thank Moria Rooney, also known as Mother of Wilde. Mother of Wilde is a small faith-based business that creates baby remembrance prints and gifts for parents of children that were lost at childbirth, miscarried, or died shortly after birth. Mother of Wilde was created by bereaved parents to honor their son, Noah Wilde, who was born silently on March 9, 2021. Their North Carolina company specializes in custom photo prints for miscarriage, stillbirth, infant, and child loss. Their products have reached bereaved moms and dads across the country and internationally. A portion of each purchase is donated to faith-based non-profits in other states, such as Angels In Waiting 91:4.

Angels In Waiting 91:4 has recently partnered with Mother of Wilde to help these grieving families. If you would happen to know of a family that could use one of these remembrance gifts in honor of their own baby, we are honored to point grieving families in the direction of Mother of Wilde. Please visit their website at www.motherofwilde.com to view their offerings.

XVI

Introduction

I am writing this book for the families who have lost infants during birth or shortly after. This is the story of Angels In Waiting 91:4 and how it all began.

Our mission statement really explains it all and what we are praying to accomplish:

"This ministry seeks to usher souls into the presence of the Holy Spirit through divine healing, deliverance, and spiritual growth through discipleship."

Beautiful angel gowns are provided for an infant's journey to meet our Lord & Savior. The angel gowns are transformed from donated wedding dresses and given to families in times of healing.

We started in October 2016, and we are still growing stronger with every passing year. Even through the COVID-19 pandemic, the ministry thrived and grew.

The stories in this book will help you to understand the depth of the issues that families who have experienced infant loss may be dealing with every day. My goal in writing this book is to show you one path to healing. Your story might be different from any of the stories I share in this book, but maybe you will be able to identify with one of the stories. There is power in sharing your story! I like to think that with every telling of your story, a link in the chain that holds you in bondage is broken. Do not be one that suffers in silence. There are families that know your pain.

Thank you for picking up this book to learn about this most unusual ministry and how it all started. More than anything else, I pray this book will give you some idea of how to move on while never forgetting your child.

Chapter One

The Ark

"Then the Lord said to Noah, 'Come into the ark, you and all your household, because I have seen that you are righteous before Me in this generation'" (Genesis 7:1).

The Lord has been speaking to me in a very unique way lately. He is giving me directions that are very clear. Christmas 2018, my husband got us tickets to go see the Ark Encounter in Kentucky. I was very excited; I'd been wanting to go for some time. We left on a Friday after a long day at work, and we arrived there around midnight. As we pulled into the hotel, I heard God say, "It's in the signs." I told my husband what I had just heard and we kind of just left it there, not thinking much about the true meaning. Of course, I journaled it as I always do because I knew it meant something, but I had no understanding at this point.

The next day we headed to the Ark Encounter. It was just amazing; as we drove up to it…it was so large and awe-inspiring. To think God spoke to one man to save humanity, and he obeyed the voice of God! Immediately, I knew I was on another mission. When we entered the ark, I heard the sound of a storm coming; I could only imagine how Noah and his family must have felt as they entered the ark many years ago. As I heard the rain and the thunder roaring, God said, "It's in the signs." Still unsure where He was going, I listened a little more carefully to His voice.

As we walked through the first deck of the ark, there before my eyes was a sign that read, "For God is not unjust to forget your work and labor of love which you have shown toward His name, in that you have ministered to saints, and do minister" (Hebrews 6:10). Immediately, I knew what He was talking about. You see, God called me to be a ministry leader for Angels In Waiting 91:4, and I had been leading the ministry for a full two years, but I was feeling overwhelmed and was not sure of the direction where God was taking us. But God had a plan all along; I just had to be obedient and listen to His voice.

We had just got on to the ark when I heard God's voice tell me to go back to the car. I was wondering to myself, *Why do we need to go back to the car when we just got here?* I was really dreading telling my husband that we needed to go back to the car. So, we got back on the shuttle bus. Then we took the long walk back to our car in a huge parking lot. Then I looked down at my cell phone in my car and saw I had missed a message from a lady back in Georgia who is a powerful, prophetic woman of God. The message said, "When you get this message, call me because I have a word from God for you!" I called her immediately, and she said, "The Lord woke me up last night to write a poem about your ministry." The poem went like this:

Angels In Waiting Ministry Team:

Maybe, we lived a few days or weeks, or we died in

our mother's womb.

We went straight to the arms of Jesus. We are not in that lonely tomb.

Thanks to you ladies who cared enough. You fashioned a garment from a wedding dress.

We were enfolded in beauty before our bodies were laid to rest.

Now we are growing and rejoicing in heaven. We are with all the other children there.

We just want to say thanks to those women who showed they care.

You blessed our parents as well by the love you showed to them.

Your reward will be in heaven, for you do it as unto Him.

[The poem was penned by Ms. Beverly Bartlett, a talented author/writer of biblically-based poems and books.]

After Ms. Bartlett read her poem that was written especially for our ministry, she prayed with us and blessed the ministry. My husband and I just looked at each other as if to say, "What just happened?" Somehow, we knew this was a trip orchestrated by God Himself. We then finished our day on the ark with God as our tour guide; all I had to do was take His hand. Those are the best adventures, anyway! When we take our hands off the wheel and let God take control. It was one of the best days ever. He continued to speak to me through all the signs that entire day.

We headed back to our hotel to spend the night and get

some dinner, and on the way, He told us where to stay. It just
so happens that when we got in our room, I started to pray to
the Lord. He told me to look out or window…there was a *big*
sign that said "Hustler." I thought, to myself, *Lord, please don't
send me there.* He spoke very loudly to me and said, "Jean, drive
around the building three times while praying over the place;
also, have your husband praying over it." We drove around
the building just as He asked us to do. I knew we had a new
mission, and we weren't done yet. Shortly thereafter, we then
went to dinner; as we sat down, my husband said, "See the guy
behind you; he has many bad spirits." I turned and looked at
the guy and said, "That's not for me," and continued to eat.
About that time, God said, "Anoint your hands and go to him."
My husband just looked at me and smiled as if to say, "Here
she goes again." I got up and walked over to his table and took
his hands in mine, and anointed him in Jesus' name. I told him
Jesus loved him, and I left.

We got in our car to head back to the hotel for the night,
and I saw a homeless man sitting on the curb; I heard God say,
"Give him the money in your wallet." I said, "Lord, I never
have cash on me." The Lord revealed Himself to me…I asked
my husband to pull over, and I looked in my wallet, and there
was some money in it. I gave it to the man and told him how
much Jesus loves him. I took his hand and prayed for him.
The man said, "Lady, I prayed to God today, and He sent an
angel to me tonight." I told him, "I am no angel, but the Lord
did send me to you. Tonight, I am only a servant of God." We
prayed together again, and I will always remember his piercing
eyes. Like I was looking into the eyes of Jesus Himself.

The Lord took me on a beautiful journey seeing the ark, but

it was much more than that…it was being in His presence and obeying Him. I pray I am able to always be near Him and that He continues to lead me. The Lord promises in Deuteronomy 31:6, "Be strong and of good courage, do not fear nor be afraid of them; for the Lord your God, He is the One who goes with you. He will not leave you nor forsake you." I don't know about you, but I find great comfort in this verse, and I am standing on His promise!

This trip to the ark was a turning point for this ministry that started two years prior. This trip was all about being obedient and doing what God told me to do.

The ministry was birthed out of my deepest pain…the birth and death of my oldest son, Brandon, to whom I have dedicated this book. Later in life, I also miscarried a set of twins. And early in life, my sister passed at a very young age. All these things were contributing factors that built one upon the other, which resulted in this area of my deepest pain. These areas of deep, deep pain resulted in my soul being terribly wounded. As an overcomer, I learned early on to push through the pain and move on to the next thing. This built strength in me but did nothing to heal the wounds because the wound was within my soul. The ministry was healing me as the wound was bleeding out, which allowed God to come into this painful place. I finally invited God into the wound, and He began to do a miracle in me by touching places I didn't want anyone to know about. With every gown that I cut out, every stitch that was sown, God was healing me.

I began having "visions" that I didn't understand for many years. The vision consisted of the most beautiful and elaborately ordained wedding dresses that I had ever seen. From these wedding dresses were angels ascending into heaven out of the wedding dresses. But these were no typical angels; these were tiny angels that resembled babies...I could see their tiny feet of all colors. I saw every race of babies. The sight was stunning to behold! The angel gowns matched precisely the wedding dress it came from. If the dress had pearls, the angel gown had pearls. If the dress was blue, so was the angel gown; if the dress was lacy, so was the angel gown. I knew God was using this as a message, but it didn't connect with my mind for the longest time.

But in the fall of 2013, we saw on social media someone who was making gowns for stillborn babies, but they were charging families for these gowns, you guessed it, made from wedding dresses. I thought about helping this organization with this service but never felt like God was leading me to work with them. To make a long story a little bit shorter, we moved back to Georgia and started attending church. In this church, we would find a home group where one of the members of the group was a NICU (neonatal intensive care unit) nurse. This nurse kept talking about needing a seamstress to make gowns for stillborn children or those that die shortly after birth. I resisted the urge to share that I could sew well, and I also resisted sharing the story of my own journey of infant loss. But my husband, after the group was over, asked me, "Have you asked God about this?" So, I asked the question to God reluctantly, and I heard an immediate reply, and He simply said, "Yes."

I texted the lady shortly thereafter, and she and her mother came to my house the following Monday. We started with a family member's dress, and neither of us had any clue what we were doing. We were ripping apart this wedding dress, tearing off beads and lace at a furious pace. That is pretty much how things started. We were later blessed by a lady who designed and sewed beautiful wedding dresses and was looking for a place to serve. She had recently moved from Tennessee and was struggling to find friends as well as a purpose. She would become an invaluable member of our tiny ministry, and God used her to design stunning angel gowns for our ministry.

From this humble beginning, a ministry was birthed. We had much to learn and lots and lots of prayers to pray, but the birthing pangs were beginning. I discovered that your assignment will always be greater than you, and your purpose is always in your greatest pain. It's hard to grow your faith inside your comfort zone, so God will often take us outside of where we are comfortable in order to grow us into the people He knows we are capable of becoming.

We definitely stepped outside of our comfort zone, and we had no idea where to begin. We didn't know how to start a ministry, we didn't have a name, and we didn't have a staff. So, everything was new, but we knew we needed to start with prayer. We prayed, and we prayed some more until the voice of God was louder than the voice of the enemy, who was telling us to quit before we even began.

The first answer to prayer was a ministry name. We chose "Angels In Waiting 91:4" because the babies are angels waiting to meet Jesus. The 91:4 is a different story. We found out that there was already a non-profit called Angels In Waiting, but it was for a different purpose than ours. As you know, heaven activates as you pray, so we prayed harder for this name. We sought legal advice and found out that we could add a number to the name and register our ministry that way. We knew the number had to be biblical, but we didn't know anything else. So, we prayed! We both prayed and came up with the same answer in Psalm 91:4.

"He shall cover you with His feathers, and under His wings you shall take refuge; His truth shall be your shield and buckler."

This verse was so fitting because the Father is covering these babies and offering His refuge. It just matched our ministry perfectly. That is how the name of the ministry was chosen, and thus, the ministry was officially birthed.

We made a social media page and posted about our need for wedding dresses, and the flood began! We were shocked about how people connected with our ministry. Volunteers started coming, and out of our meetings, a Bible study began. People were not only coming to volunteer, but they were also coming to meet Jesus in a very profound and unusual way. The Bible study and evangelistic outreach were completely unplanned, but we just listened to the voice of God and acted on His Word. God amazed me every day during this time…He still does! For example, I went to a Christian bookstore to find an appropriate Bible study. I really wanted to teach something from Beth Moore, but I kept coming back to this book that had a picture of a needle and thread. The title of that study was called *Seamless* by Angie Smith. As it turned out, Angie and her husband lost their third child due to infant loss. You can't make this stuff up. God literally wanted me to teach this study, and I had no idea that she had lost a child too. That was the first Bible study for the volunteers that showed up every week. From here, the ministry just grew and grew. We are continuing to grow to this day.

A prophetess, who is a dear friend of mine and part of

the ministry, told me that this ministry was like a gas station. People will come to fill up their tanks and leave. Others will like the "gas" so much that they continue to return to get filled up. Others may only visit occasionally when their tank is running low. This is how the Lord has used me during this time. Before all this began, I once prayed, "Lord, use me in whatever way You see fit," and that is exactly what He has done.

In short, that's the background of how Angels In Waiting 91:4 came to be. In the pages and chapters that follow, you will hear the stories behind the wedding dresses and the impact the "angel gowns" have had upon the families affected by the loss of their children.

Most of these families suffer in silence. Yet one in four women experiences the loss of a child. This ministry was created in part to offer some sort of healing for those that have lost an infant and to let them know that they are not alone and that people care. There is hope and healing on the other side of brokenness.

Chapter Two

Miles and Miles before She Goes

"And begged him to let the sick just touch the edge of his cloak, and all who touched it were healed" (Matthew 14:36, NIV).

Dresses started coming into my home, where I felt a little overwhelmed. We had a pattern, but surely, I was not the one to cut and sew these angel gowns together. The Lord woke me up one night and said, "Make me an angel gown out of the presidential gown." I sat up in my bed, wondering what He wanted from me? *Lord, I am listening to You, but I am not sure it's me you want; this is out of my expertise.* But I got up and did as the Lord had asked me to do; I cut out the pattern from the exact wedding dress He told me to, and I began to sew it all together. It was not the prettiest angel dress we had made because the lady that does the girls' angel gowns does amazing work. I finished the angel gown, and I heard Him say, "This one is for someone very special."

This angel gown had a very special assignment. There was a baby who went to heaven, and her mother walked miles back to the hospital to choose an angel gown out of several to bury her little girl in. She also picked out a tiny blanket that a precious lady that volunteered with us sewed with flannel that had tiny pink roses on it and a crocheted edge all around that just happened to speak to this mother. The roses on the blanket were identical to the roses she was doing the baby's room in. The blanket reminded her of the nursery her baby was going to have. I want you to see how Jesus is in the details of our lives, even in death.

The volunteer who made this blanket was also a mother of an angel baby and the mother of another one of our volunteers, Kay Wilson. We will come back to Kay later. Ironically, shortly after making this blanket and the mother choosing this blanket, the volunteer also went home to be with the Lord. Jesus has a way of knitting (pardon the pun) all the details of our life together. He is in the details! These details are often things we could not possibly imagine, let alone figure out how they fit into the bigger picture. But the Lord not only sees the big picture, but He also sees the minute details that hold it all together for our good.

The gown this precious mother chose was the very same gown that God Himself chose for this mother's little girl. The same gown that God had me design in the middle of the night. The nurse that helped this young mother through the loss of her baby said she laid out all twenty-five gowns for this mother (placing the gown God had told me to design on the bottom of the pile). The mother went straight to the gown that God chose for her baby, and that was the gown in which her child met Jesus.

"But those who wait on the Lord Shall renew their strength;

They shall mount up with wings like eagles, They shall run and not be weary, They shall walk and not faint" (Isaiah 40:31).

Kay Wilson is one of our treasured volunteers, a dear friend, and one of the very first volunteers. She is also an artist that designed a painting for Angels In Waiting 91:4, which will be proudly displayed in our dedicated space for Angels In Waiting 91:4.

I asked Kay to provide some words of her own to describe what Angels In Waiting 91:4 has meant to her...

"I am a Jesus follower, wife, mother of three, grandmother of five, and a nurse. I am no different than anyone else, searching for my passion and something to fill the hours during the 2020 pandemic. I decided to take online watercolor classes, and this cover is a result of that venture. In 1980 I began my nursing career, and twenty-two years ago, I found one of my passions—caring for babies in the NICU. I have loved caring for these tiny warriors, helping them on their journey home. Sometimes that journey is home to loving parents, and sometimes it is to meet the Father. I have laughed and cried and prayed with and over families and have been so blessed by these experiences.

"Five years ago, I met Jean and became involved with Angels In Waiting 91:4. It has changed me and my walk with Jesus. I have seen the Lord's hand at work, and while that never surprises me, I am always amazed at His loving kindness, and now He knits life's stories together. For example, when I was three, my sister, Betty Lynn, was born sleeping. My mother often spoke of Betty Lynn and told the story of her birth and her grieving. My mom became a part of Angels for a short time until her health wouldn't allow it. I believe she finally found healing some sixty years later, making blankets and being a part of this ministry where she could share her story and grief. Prior to her passing, God took her to heaven and allowed her to see Betty Lynn, and she was able to share this story with me. She told me how magnificent heaven looked and how beautiful my baby sister looked. What a sweet blessing I received, sharing this journey with my sweet mama. She passed a few days later, and I was given the peace that passes all understanding. I think life is like a beautiful tapestry, woven together by the Father with the threads of happiness, heartache, love, and joy. This book is a true testament to that. I pray this book somehow gives comfort in knowing one day you will see your child in all their glory, happy and whole with the Father."

This next story was a wedding dress that came to us through an amazing story of twenty years of silence. This young lady was engaged to be married. She had bought her wedding dress and was excited about the rehearsal and the wedding, but on the night of the rehearsal, she was in a terrible car accident. At the age of twenty-three, this accident took the life of her soon-to-be husband and placed her in twenty years of coma. After almost two decades of lying in a coma, the parents and family decided to let her go home to heaven.

It was right before Christmas that her wedding dress was donated to our ministry, and she was going home that same month. We prayed over the wedding dress with the family and comforted them. Praying that, in some small way, this would help to bring healing to a deep place of hurt. This was such a hard day for all of us. This precious lady was released into the hands of our heavenly Father. It was truly a glorious day! I pray this family received the love of Jesus as they entered our world and our ministry. This ministry is not for the faint of heart, and it's not always as fun and easy as it seems when you have so many stories of lives we are touching.

There were many beautiful angel gowns made from her beautifully never-worn wedding dress. I pray she got a glimpse of our hands as they ripped her dress apart and made such delicate little angel gowns for Jesus.

In this young woman's obituary, which we received a few months after the funeral, was a beautiful poem written by an unknown author entitled "The Final Flight":

Don't grieve for me, for now I'm free.
I'm following the path God laid for me.
I took His hand when I heard His call,
I turned my back and left it all.
Perhaps my time seemed all too brief,
Don't lengthen it now with undue grief.
Lift your heart and share with me,
God wanted me now, He set me free.

Truer words have never been spoken. There is so much depth and healing in these words. True freedom comes when we are in the arms of Jesus! This young lady received her freedom after all those years of silence. Her life on this earth may have ended sooner than she would have hoped, but she never knew the joy that was awaiting her in heaven.

Her family came back to deliver the box of angel gowns, which were made from their daughter's wedding dress, to the same hospital where she laid in a coma for so many years. We never heard from them again, but we know we operated as Jesus' hands and feet to help usher in healing to this devastated family.

The Lord even began giving me little details about how to function. We found a perfect box at a local retailer that had Psalm 91:4 on the box. We began buying these boxes until we could no longer get them. Then we designed one with our own logo. In these delivery boxes, we place twenty-five gowns. Why twenty-five gowns? Why not ten or even fifty? The simple answer is because the Lord told me to put twenty-five gowns in the boxes. The biblical meaning of the number twenty-five is "grace upon grace." God spoke to me and told me that He was placing grace upon grace to the families that receive these gowns. My son came and told me, "Do you know what twenty-five means biblically?" He then told me it means grace upon grace. God will use those who don't know Him yet to deliver His messages of confirmation.

Once the angel gowns are complete, at the end of each Transformation Tuesday, the team gathers all gowns made that day, and each gown is prayed over and anointed with oil. We pray that God would usher in healing to the families that receive the gowns. Every part of the process is bathed in prayer!

One thing I discovered early on as we embarked upon this journey is to pray about everything and give Him all the glory! That is exactly what we have done! This is His ministry on loan to me to manage and do as He tells me to do. He told us the ministry must be nameless and faceless, giving Him all the glory. We have been obedient to this dictate from the beginning.

I briefly mentioned how God is in the details of our lives at the beginning of this chapter. He has certainly been in the details of this ministry. When this all began, I didn't have a clue what was involved in starting a non-profit ministry. But

God seemed to have all the right connections in place at every step of the way. Often, He has provided things we didn't know we needed, or He would put us into contact with people that seemed to know exactly what we were looking for at that point in time. Or sometimes, He knocks over a domino that causes everything else to fall into place.

I really love how my husband describes how God is in the tiniest of details. My husband says that our lives are like a beautiful cut diamond with lots of different facets. It's all the different planes created by those facets which show off the internal beauty of the diamond. The light that reflects off the many different planes created by the cuts is what creates the beauty. The master gemologist deftly designs the cut of the diamond and knows just where to cut it to show off the beauty and shimmer of the gem. The cuts being made by the master gemologist might seem rather scary to the person who is not adept at cutting the stone. But those cuts create the different planes and prisms that reflect the light, which causes the shimmer in the stones.

Like a master gemologist, God knows exactly where we need to be "cut" to reflect the most light…His light. Ironically, these cuts also make us stronger. But every cut works in cooperation with all the other cuts to create a unique beauty that can only come from within us. This is perfectly described in the Bible in the book of Romans, chapter eight:

"And we know that all things work together for good to those who love God, to those who are the called according to His purpose" (Romans 8:28).

A diamond is a lump of coal that has come under extreme pressure for many, many years, far under the crust of the earth.

After the pressure on the lump of coal forms the stone, there is still no beauty in it. In fact, many people may not even be able to recognize a diamond and simply toss it aside like a worthless rock. It takes someone who knows how to identify the raw diamond and where to take the stone to ultimately reveal its beauty and its worth.

God knows your worth and can see the beauty within you.

So, God will even use the bad things in our lives, such as the loss of a baby, for our own good. It is terribly painful to go through this experience. But if we allow God to do what only He can do, He will ultimately turn it around for our good. This won't be a comfort to you now, but later down the line, God will bring to your remembrance how He strengthened you through all of this. But we have to cooperate with the process of healing and cooperate with God. There is always a bigger picture at play, but we fail to see it because we are too close to it. Grief is the price we pay for love. Think about all those we have loved and the pain that comes about when there is a final separation. When we can step back from the pain, and it will likely take years, we will discover that we are a different person with more strength and more love to give to others as a result of our pain. God uses all the details…good and bad.

Chapter Three

It's Not My Fault

"Blessed are those who mourn, For they shall be comforted" (Matthew 5:4).

A lady brought the wedding dress that she wanted to donate due to a divorce. We began to pray over her and her dress, and she began to weep and tell us her story. Her marriage ended due to an affair with her best friend, which resulted in a baby for the new family. She began to tell us her wedding day was one of the happiest days of her life, and now it feels like the worst. She was heartbroken and unable to forgive either of them.

The Lord woke me up that night, telling me to make an angel gown out of this lady's dress for one of His angels. I got up and started cutting out the pattern and then sewed it together. This gown was not our normal size, it was slightly larger, but I couldn't understand what I was doing or really what I was seeing. I showed the angel gown to the volunteers as they came that week for Transformation Tuesday, and they all said it was a little bigger, but we just blew it off and went on with our day as usual. Another sweet volunteer was knitting booties, and she noticed these booties were also an odd shape. One bootie was a little bigger than the other.

She told me, "I really don't know why these are so small and why one was bigger than the other."

I just smiled and said, "God knows." And I said, "We can just set them up as a display on the shelf."

A few days later, the same lady that donated the wedding dress called me to ask me if we had an angel gown that she could have due to the death of an angel on her ex-husband's side of her family. I told her the story of God waking me up a few nights before to make an angel gown out of her wedding dress, and she came to get that gown. She came by and held the angel gown in her hand with such amazement and asked, "By chance do you have any booties?"

I smiled and said, "Why yes, I only have booties that we use for a display on the shelf because they are an odd size!"

She said, "That's okay; I'll take them anyway."

God knows all things, and He puts all things together for us even when it makes no sense to us. I gave them to her, and off she went, with tears in her eyes and covered in many prayers.

The baby was full term. A friend of mine, who is a NICU nurse, was doubting if the angel gown would fit this full-term baby. I told her, "God used me to make that size of angel gown, so it will fit." A few days later, I got a phone call from this precious lady to tell me the angel gown fit this little angel perfectly, and so did the extra small set of booties. Even though the baby was full-term, it had very small feet, with one a little bigger than the other, which fit inside the provided booties perfectly. This just showed me that God is in the details of every little thing we do. He knew better even when our flesh wanted to get in the way. I am reminded of the words of Prophet Jeremiah where he says, "Before I formed you in the womb I knew you" (Jeremiah 1:5).

When obedience happens, everything falls into place. I don't need to understand what God tells me to do; I just need to do it. He is the creator and master of all things…I have a small job to do for Him. Peace, love, and forgiveness came back into this broken family through the death of this little angel. God is willing and able to take a tragic moment and bring healing.

Although the divorce was not this woman's fault—it was her husband's sin after all—God used the death of a baby to bring healing to all involved. Forgiveness was necessary, but it only became possible when she let go of the pain and released her ex-husband from the charge she held against him. The need for forgiveness came about as the result of a tiny life going home to be with the Lord.

Often a wound is placed by the devil in an effort to take you out. You must put on your full armor daily, as it says in Ephesians 6, and stay at the feet of Jesus. It is out of your brokenness that you discover what you have to offer to others.

Another dress came in the mail one day with a letter that I must share with you. This lady wrote a letter telling us that when she was four or five years old, she lived in Asia, and the windows had bars on them to prevent robbers. She was climbing on the bars and slipped, landing on her pregnant aunt, which was several months pregnant at the time, causing her to lose the baby. She went on to say, "I know this is not my fault, but I still can't help but feel guilty about it." In that Asian culture, this event brought shame to herself and to her family. She was disowned by her family because her aunt was unable to have children as a result of the accident. This lady stated in the letter that she hoped to gain healing from this event as a result of her sacrificing something important to her in exchange for the life that was lost. We never heard the rest of the story from this point.

One thing we know for certain is that the devil tries to keep us in bondage and shame. He was and is a liar from the start. Both these precious ladies were held in bondage from the past. I am here to tell you Jesus Christ came to set the captives free.

> The Spirit of the Lord is upon Me, Because He has anointed Me To preach the gospel to the poor; He has sent Me to heal the brokenhearted, To proclaim liberty to the captives And recovery of sight to the blind, To set at liberty those who are oppressed.
>
> Luke 4:18

We only need to trust Him, and He will do the rest. Jesus came to give us life and life more abundantly, as it says in the book of John. "The thief does not come except to steal, and to kill, and to destroy. I have come that they may have life, and that they may have it more abundantly" (John 10:10). We do have a part to play in cooperating with the process and being obedient to His calling upon us, however. But Jesus will do the heavy lifting.

The healing that must come for these two ladies can only come through Jesus. We must remember,

> For we do not wrestle against flesh and blood, but against principalities, against powers, against the rulers of the darkness of this age, against spiritual hosts of wickedness in the heavenly places.

Ephesians 6:12

As we stated in chapter one, this ministry is built upon prayer and obedience to His Word. We believe that we are a healing and deliverance ministry, first and foremost. Every gown is spiritually cleansed upon arrival and anointed with oil to assure the recipients receive a truly blessed gown to send their child home. The key to any ministry is prayer!

These gowns may be the door through which the people touched by them meet Jesus. We keep that at the forefront of our minds as we design and sew these gowns together.

So, the stories above may be a story of contrast and comparison. One family received healing through the giving of a donated wedding dress. While the second lady, we are unsure of the results. This is where we must trust Jesus to do the heavy lifting. The gown in the second instance may not have brought healing in and of itself. But could have simply been an open door to the gospel. God can use anything and anyone to accomplish His work!

Wedding dresses can be donated in person at our Angels In Waiting 91:4 headquarters on Transformation Tuesday. People can come by and drop off the donated gowns between our working hours of 9 a.m. to 3 p.m. We receive the dress, and we always like to hear the stories behind the donations. Sometimes these are stories of triumph, and sometimes, these are stories of tragedy. We will then pray over the dress with the family, blessing both the dress and the family in addition to the blessing of the angel gowns that will be made from the dress. This is critical! Many times, these angel gowns go to the exact families that God has intended for these gowns. We have heard many stories of how these gowns have touched families.

God will use even tragic times to bring about His will and purpose. To be clear here, God does not cause these things to happen for His purposes, but He can use these events or difficulties to accomplish His greater glory.

Look at the story of Job as a perfect example. Job was depicted as a devoted man of God, a husband, and a father. In fact, God the Father held Job up as a model citizen. Job was faithful and devoted to God in all he did. If you know anything about Job, then you know the story of how Satan entered God's chambers in the second heaven after going to and fro throughout the earth. God praised Job for his upright behavior. But then Satan told God that Job was only on his best behavior because God had blessed him with prosperity. Job had the model life; he was happily married and had ten children that loved him dearly as the patriarch of the family. God permits Satan to strip Job of everything in order to prove Job's faithfulness to God. So, Satan takes all of Job's wealth, all of his children, and his marriage. Job had nothing left! Then Job's friends come along and enter into a debate with Job about why this destruction had come upon him. His friends did nothing to comfort Job over his losses. Meanwhile, Job still refused to blame God for his predicament. Ultimately, God Himself steps in to remind all of them of His great power but doesn't really come to

Job's defense. Job was reminded of God's sovereignty, and God blesses Job for his faithfulness by giving him double what he lost. He also gave him a new family.

Job went through far more than any of us would have to endure. But Job remained faithful to God, trusting in God's sovereignty and honoring God instead of blaming or cursing God. We don't often react the same way when life turns out less than what we expect. This is especially true in the affluent Western world.

Those in the Middle East have a far better understanding of ancient ways, and they do a much better job of honoring the ancient paths. Of course, we don't have any way of knowing if God allows us to be tested like Job, but we can react to the circumstances of our own lives in a similar manner to Job.

Yes, we mourn the loss; that is a natural part of life. But we cannot stay in that place of defeat and loss. Like Job, we can overcome the pain of the wounds inflicted upon us if we put our focus on God instead of keeping our pain bottled up. We must learn to accept the loss and move into what God has in store for us. God's plans are far better than we could ever imagine if only we stay within His will for our lives.

But that's the trick when we find ourselves in a place of horrendous circumstances. We will blame God or others for our loss when sometimes it is simply part of living in a fallen world. Staying within God's will can be a very difficult challenge in circumstances like the loss of a child. But God can and will take the most difficult of times and turn them around for our own good. It will never replace the loss but will ease the pain and help us to be able to cope with life.

So, in your place of loss or tragedy, keep your focus on the sovereignty of God and allow Him to ease your pain!

Chapter Four

I'll Hold You until We Meet Again

"I will praise You, for I am fearfully and wonderfully made; Marvelous are Your works, And that my soul knows very well" (Psalm 139:14).

I was twenty years old; I was married and expecting my first baby! I was so very excited! We picked out the furniture for the room, painted it, and we had the baby shower! This was all so real and beautiful until I started feeling bad.

There seemed to be some complications, but I thought everything would be okay. I was hoping to go to see a specialist on the following Monday, but I was experiencing some bleeding, and I was not feeling my best. It was Sunday, and I told my little brother, who was nine years old at the time…that my back really hurt. Thinking nothing of it, I tried to ignore it, but he was smarter than me, and he called my best friend to come to check on me. She came to the house and had me go to the hospital for a quick check. I remember seeing my little brother's sweet little face in the elevator as we went up to the maternity floor. This would be the last time I saw my brother until we were standing by a tiny grave in the rain.

I was supposed to see a specialist on Monday, but Jesus had other plans for my baby and me. Sunday night, I went into premature labor and gave birth to a one-and-a-half-pound baby boy who was born alive but only lived for a very short time on this earth. The first place he opened his precious little eyes was in heaven, seeing Jesus face to face. What a glorious time for him, but for me, I was lost, sad, and very confused. I wondered why had this happened to me? What kind of God takes a baby from his mother? This would be the beginning of many difficult years…it felt like I was living in hell at the time.

I remember the doctor and nurse were in the room with me, and they said, "It's time for the baby to arrive." I am having my baby *boy*! I was scared and happy all at once. I gave birth to my first baby, but I never heard him cry. Then I heard the doctor say, "He's alive." I thought to myself, *Well, of course, he's alive.* Then there was a lot of chaos in the room and a lot of noise, but still no sound of a baby's cry.

I looked into the nurse's eyes, and she whispered, "He was just too small."

What does that mean? My heart couldn't accept these words!

I was taken back to my room, where it was very quiet. People coming in and out with questions being thrown around like, "Do you want us to dispose of the body, or do you want a Christian burial?" "What do you want?" I only wanted my baby! I was not able to think correctly! My dad spoke up and said, "We will bury him." I was so grateful at that moment because I was unable to even think clearly.

My parents picked out clothes for him to be buried in. It

was a tiny white gown with little blue booties and rattles on it. He also had a little baby blue blanket to cover him. Brandon was only one pound and six ounces, so the gown was way too big because they didn't make gowns for premature babies at that time.

My aunt worked at the hospital Brandon was born and was aware of the problems I was experiencing with Brandon's birth. She stood there with the funeral director as they placed Brandon in the hearse to take him to the funeral home. She told me that the funeral director carried him, in his hand, with a small white cloth covering him. I am eternally grateful for what she did for us. The compassion and love she showed for us during such a difficult time will always be carried in my heart.

We did have a funeral which was beautiful, and Jesus really came through for me and comforted me in a million different ways. The rain was pouring, and I remember standing on that graveside, looking at a tiny blue casket that held my son in it. I remember seeing one of my brothers who dug my son's grave as his eyes touched mine. I can never thank him enough for such an act of love. We bonded in a new way that day. He later was the one who placed the dirt over that little, tiny blue casket for his very own nephew. It's funny how families can fight and argue, but when tragedy comes, family always seems to come to the rescue. I will always be so grateful for my family; they all came through in a way they never had before. My family made all the decisions, as my husband and I were too heartbroken to even think about such things.

There is healing on the other side of brokenness. I was wondering how does my heart begin to heal in this area? When the dirt was placed over that tiny grave, I wondered, *How do I do*

this? Where is God in this? I can't see Him…I can't feel Him. I ran
from Jesus at this point. I was so mad at Him, and yet He continued to love me. What kind of God does this? God knew all
things and was preparing my heart for this future ministry. He
would birth this ministry out of me many years later. Brandon
was chosen by the God who made heaven and earth, so I had
to learn to rest in Him and His Word. My son is resting in the
arms of Jesus, and there is no better place than that.

But Brandon was not the only loss of a loved one I have had
to experience. At the age of three, I lost my sister, who was only
eighteen months old when she left my life, at far too young of
an age. At this point in my life, she was my best friend. Her
death was a true tragedy of epic proportions. I also miscarried
a set of twin girls after my youngest son was born. I've also lost
grandparents who helped raise me. They were my everything.
So, to say that I am well acquainted with the loss of loved ones
is an extreme understatement.

After Brandon's death, the hospital gave me a verse from
the Bible that states, "I will praise You, for I am fearfully and
wonderfully made; Marvelous are Your works, And that my soul
knows very well" (Psalm 139:14). I held onto this verse in my
heart, and when I needed hope, I would pull it out.

I know now that all God's creation testifies to His power
and majesty! I realized I was not being punished by God, but
rather He chose me to be a mother to an angel baby. This was
my assignment. Your assignment will always be greater than
you. To hand my baby boy over to Jesus was my greatest pain.
Your purpose is always in your greatest pain.

I had never known pain like this before in my life. It cut so
deep, but I soon learned in Revelation 21:5…that He makes all

things new. My hope was that He would bring something good out of this pain. He did just as He says in His Word, in Romans 8:28, "And we know that all things work together for good to those who love God, to those who are the called according to His purpose."

I knew I loved Him, and I wanted to be obedient to His purpose. The pain remained real, but I knew that Jesus keeps His promises. Going home to a house with blue flowers all over the place was so very painful. I asked my aunt to please just throw them all away! She did, and that was such a wonderful help during this time.

This was a terribly confusing time for me. You see, I knew of Jesus, but I didn't have a relationship with Him at this point in my life. So, I couldn't understand how He could turn this terrible situation into anything good. But He did! Angels In Waiting 91:4 was birthed out of my deepest pain. As I stated before, your kingdom's purpose will always be found in your deepest pain.

I think the thing that hurt me the most was it seemed like this was a normal thing, and I should just get over it and move on. I heard people say, "Oh, it wasn't even a baby; she is young enough she will have other children." And the most hurtful of all was, "Why bury it when the hospital can take care of it for free?" People need to remember during this time of loss to be gentle with their words because they can place a lifetime of wounds in a person. These wounds eventually turn into scars, but not until the Savior heals them. I carry many scars from word curses that were spoken over me. It has taken me many years to work through these wounds. Please be careful what you speak over people because it can take a lifetime to clear up.

When a mother loses her child, those are the last words she wants to hear, especially by people who are supposed to love her. It is like being in a very dark place all alone. Only Jesus can heal this kind of pain. It has been a long hard road, but healing did come to me. Brandon's birthday is celebrated in heaven with Jesus, but not one year goes by that I don't wonder what he would have been like. One day, I will celebrate with him in heaven.

I was praying many years later, after having four sons of my own, and I asked God, "Why did You take my son?" He simply replied, "Because there is a lady in heaven who was never able to have any children, and she is loving on your son until you get here." I was so grateful for these precious words. He then said her name was Toni with an "I." I truly had no idea what He was talking about, but I journaled it and went on with my life. It was several weeks later when a box came in the mail, and as I opened it, I could feel the presence of the Lord. There was a beautiful wedding dress with a note attached that read:

> I'm sure most people who donate these dresses do not write letters. My husband and I have prayed over this, and our hearts are swelling with joy to pass our daughter's dress to this organization. God bless you for having such loving and caring people who would take the time to make these angel gowns. God blessed us with two beautiful and loving girls. Both have been called to heaven. This dress belonged to Toni, our first child. I just wanted you to know she's in heaven smiling. You see, she could never have children. I'm sure when these little angels get to heaven, she will greet them with loving arms and a beautiful smile. Love

and God bless you all for doing God's work. Toni's
dad & mom.

As we worked on Toni's dress, the Holy Spirit was so present. It was one of the most beautiful moments I've ever known.
Oh, how He brings it all together when we become obedient to
Him! Jesus requires our obedience. Following Him will cost you
everything. You must come to the end of yourself to really get
to know all Jesus has for you.

How does one heal from such a devastating thing? The only
answer I have found to this question is Jesus. He is the only
way anyone can ever recover from the pain of having your heart
ripped out of your chest. God must have known so well this
pain as He watched His only begotten Son as He hung on that
cross, with blood running down Jesus' face, and as He cried out,
"It is finished." God almighty endured that same kind of pain
you and I have suffered as we, too, have lost our own children.
There is such hope in that we can heal from this, but we must
turn our eyes to Jesus Christ, so healing can begin.

I'll ask you a question for you to ponder, have you given
this pain over to the only one who can walk with you through
it? If not, I encourage you to do so now. Say this short little
prayer and open yourself up to be vulnerable before your Savior.
Jesus is such a gentleman, and He will only come where He is
invited. "Lord Jesus, come into this wound right now and walk
with me through this most difficult time and bring healing to
my broken heart. I love You, Lord, and I trust in Your ways.
Amen!" Now, let the healing begin!

As we deliver these boxes to the hospitals, these gowns have
been prayed over, and we ask God for healing for families like

mine.

We deliver boxes literally all over the world, including to Israel, Canada, and Australia. We currently have delivered boxes in twenty-nine states. Usually, our volunteers deliver the boxes when they go on trips somewhere. But sometimes, we get requests for angel gowns from social media or through our website or newsletters. We also get requests from donors of wedding dresses to deliver boxes to the hospitals of their choice. We simply ask for pictures and a business card so we can track where our boxes are delivered.

If you would like to deliver a box or make a wedding dress donation, please reach out to our ministry through social media or our website at www.angelsinwaiting914.com.

Chapter Five

I Set in Remembrance of You

"Surely he will never be shaken; The righteous will be an everlasting remembrance" (Psalm 112:6).

Often in life, we are handed surprises that we couldn't in a million years make up the story. This is the case for our next story.

This young woman was a NICU nurse who knew our ministry well, having firsthand knowledge of what we do. She loved our ministry and decided to donate her wedding dress in memory of her little girl that was born sleeping. This mother struggled mightily with the death of her daughter, never really finding healing for this deep wound in her life. While she had a son previously, which was a big comfort in itself, even the love of her son and husband was not able to fulfill the void left behind by the death of her baby girl.

Her wedding dress was donated almost five years after her baby girl passed away. She was hoping to deliver the box of angel gowns on her baby's fifth birthday. We transformed the dress into beautiful angel gowns, which she delivered to the hospital where she worked in the unit where she lost her child. She kept five of the angel gowns in memory of her baby. She was thrilled to receive these gowns on her baby girl's birthday! This deep wound was enough of a surprise for anyone, but God had another plan for this devastated young woman and her family.

In 2020, while most of the world was locked down due to the Coronavirus, this frontline worker was afflicted with COVID-19. She struggled to survive but was unable to overcome the pandemic. Fortunately, this young mother was reunited with her baby girl in heaven. I say "fortunately" because she was never able to heal from the loss of her baby girl but was reunited with her much sooner than she anticipated, for that I am certain.

While her husband and son were left behind, they too have the hope of being reunited someday! We must always remember that God's plans are not our plans, and His thoughts are much higher than our thoughts. While this family experienced tragedy on multiple levels, they must put their hope in Jesus Christ alone. Jesus is our Savior, our redeemer, and our best friend! He sticks closer than a brother and is always present if you are a believer in Him.

The next story was of a lady in South Carolina who drove to Georgia to donate her daughter-in-law's wedding dress. She was very excited because she was about to have her first grandbaby. About a week went by when this grandmother-to-be called us and told us her grandbaby would have severe birth defects. If the baby was carried full-term, it would be born without a fully developed brain. Her son and daughter-in-law decided to have the baby instead of aborting the child. While the grandmother was a Christian, the rest of the family was pretty much church attenders and did not have much of a relationship with Jesus Christ at the time.

However, after carrying this baby to term and ultimately having to return the child back to the arms of Jesus, the entire family developed a deep love of Christ.

While we deeply love our family, our spouse, and friends, we have never known a love like that of Jesus Christ unless we cultivate a relationship with Him. You may be asking yourself, "How do I get this relationship with a Savior that loves me so deeply (unlike anything I've ever known)?" Like any relationship, it largely takes time spent getting to know Him. This is done mostly in prayer and in reading the Word of God. The Bible is our source for knowing our Savior's character and personality. Once we accept Jesus as our Savior, we then have the Holy Spirit residing within us, making us a new creation. This is how we grow deeper in love with Him! His love surrounds us like a warm blanket on a cold winter's night. He knows the deepest recesses of our hearts and heals the broken places…if we will allow Him to.

I am reminded of the apostle Paul's words in 1 Thessalonians 3:6–8, where Timothy brought back word of the faith, love, and affection of the church of Thessalonica for Paul.

> But now that Timothy has come to us from you, and brought us good news of your faith and love, and that you always have good remembrance of us, greatly desiring to see us, as we also to see you— therefore, brethren, in all our affliction and distress we were comforted concerning you by your faith. For now we live, if you stand fast in the Lord.

The church missed Paul and greatly desired to see him again. Paul says he was comforted by their faith and the fact that they stood fast in the Lord.

Like us, when we lose a loved one, sometimes too early in life, if we stand fast in the Lord and maintain our faith in Him, we have the hope of seeing Him and our loved ones in heaven. Apart from placing our trust and faith in Him, we have no hope at all.

In many families that have experienced the loss of a baby, the daddies are often an afterthought. All eyes and words of comfort are mostly directed to the mother. But the truth is all family members are affected by this kind of loss. We did not want to lose sight of the other family members.

As the ministry matured more and more, we realized that somehow, we had neglected the daddies of the families that have lost a baby at birth or shortly thereafter. We went to an event where a dad spoke to us about the loss of their child, where he educated us on the grief of the daddy. We began praying for the daddies more earnestly than we had before. Because the daddies often suffer in silence. Many of the dads have no one to talk to about their loss, and they bear the burden of the entire family, all the while trying to deal with the loss of a life that was cut far too short. Dads need to hold the family together during these times of loss, so they often do not share their own grief with others. Dad's focus goes to the mother to try to help her heal, all the while neglecting his own need for healing.

One way we have decided to honor daddies is by using their neckties to make the boy angel gowns. We use neckties to make the vest, a bowtie, a tiny necktie, and buttons for the boy gowns. Our prayer is that by honoring the dads of an infant that has passed away that we can bring healing to the entire family. Daddies matter too!

When we lose a loved one, either young or old, especially when the death is premature, it leaves us with a sense of void in our lives. There is a grieving process for certain, but we can get stuck in that grief if we allow it to consume us. Sometimes we may even want to die ourselves in order to be free from the pain of doing life without someone we cared for so deeply. A proper perspective is needed in these times. In fact, I would say that a proper perspective is critical at this time in our life. It could even mean a life-or-death situation for us...spiritually or physically.

Life can come at us fast. Let's face it, more times than we care to admit, we don't expect to lose someone in life before their time is up. Death is often unexpected. We live in a broken world, where the ruler of this world has taken control because of the disobedience of fallen mankind. However, that was not God's intention at the time of creation. He made man to have dominion over the earth, care for it, and to prosper in it. In fact, death was not part of God's original design. We were created to be immortal, but pride, stubbornness, and disobedience led us to a place where all things have a beginning and an end. Death, whether premature or not, is an end. Some lead lives that are well-lived, while others never get a chance to live their life at all. There is no rhyme or reason to it all. Life and death happen as a result of the fall. The devil comes to steal our life and our purpose. The devil's desire is for us not to fulfill our God-given purpose and to steal our joy. We have a choice to make in difficult times, like the death of a child. Will we move forward into our destiny, or will we succumb to the wiles of the enemy? The choice is ours to make.

In chapter three, I wrote about how our battle is not against flesh and blood but against powers and principalities of this dark age (Ephesians 6:12). In the preceding verse, it says, "Put on the whole armor of God, that you may be able to stand against the wiles of the devil" (Ephesians 6:11). The word for wiles in the original Greek language is *methodeia*. Loosely translated, it means the different means, plans, and schemes used to deceive, entrap, enslave, and ruin the souls of man.

So how are we supposed to move on when we feel like we can't even get out of bed? I remember after the birth and death of my son, my body displayed all the effects of the birth, but there was no life; only the pain of loss remained. All the plans had been laid for a new life to join with mine. Even my body was still producing hormones and milk that said a new life was coming. But the new life never manifested…only the pain of loss was still present. I woke from bed one morning needing to go to the bathroom, to take a shower, to somehow try to live my life again. Someone had left a Bible open in my room, and as I walked by, I simply closed the Bible as if to say to God, "Where were You in all of this?" "Why did You not save my baby boy?" Someone cared enough to point me to where life could be found again, but I couldn't receive it at this point in my life. Everybody else was moving forward, including my husband. But I was stuck in a very dark place. I blamed God, but it wasn't His fault. My perspective was all wrong. I rebelled against all things to do with God. But it wasn't God that took my baby; it was the enemy. The devil sought to knock me off the path and cause me to live in a constant state of heartache and pain.

But because of the devil's plans laid up against us, we must be strong in the Lord and in the power of His might, not our own. If we try to live according to our own strength, we will never get to where God wants us to be…we will never achieve our own God-ordained destiny. The devil will use whatever means necessary to do his bidding. We need God's power and strength to be able to stand against the enemy. But sometimes, we simply need to withstand the attack on our life and our destiny. God has abundant life designed for us (see John 10:10), the attack can be brutal and unrelenting, but we must be able to withstand the ferocity of the attack.

Strength can only come through adversity. The adversity will empower us for the next steps in our life. As a people, we underestimate our ability to withstand the trials of this life. Losing a child is one of the most difficult trials anybody would have to endure. It's not natural to bury a child. A parent was never designed to outlive their children. But God gives us difficult trials to prepare us for the journey ahead. You can endure more than you think you can with His help!

For me, God brought that open Bible back around to me. He brought back the words of my grandmother spoken to give life and instruct me in the way that I should go. Her words were always based on the Word of God. Like God's Word, her words always led me back to Him. I remember old bluegrass gospel music playing in my grandmother's house and me asking why she played that old music. She simply told me that one day she hoped I would understand. So, after walking through the pain and failing through life in my own effort, I turned it all over to Him and surrendered my will to His. In effect, I exchanged my life for His.

If you haven't done so already, find someone who can help you walk through your journey from loss to healing. Everything the enemy intends for evil; God will turn it around for your good. The process can be long and difficult; it was for me. I rebelled against God even though I was still sitting in a church pew. I was still angry at God. I was angry over the loss of my own child and from a painful childhood. On the outside, I looked like I had it all together, but I certainly did not have a relationship with Jesus. If I had died during this time, I was bound on a path straight to hell. I would have never had the opportunity to see my son again. When I truly found Jesus and invited Him into my heart, that all changed. I found my Savior, or should I say He found me? Jesus was never lost, but I was. We need to implant this into our souls. Jesus is the same yesterday, today, and forever. God continued to seek me even when I wasn't seeking Him. I pray that you don't find yourself in my example. I pray that you entrust your life to Him, and He will make you strong. Remember, it's not by your own effort that you find strength. True strength can only come through Jesus Christ.

God has a plan marked out for us. We still can choose our own path, but if we follow His path, we will come to certain healing. You see, the day my son was born, and Jesus took Him home…Jesus already knew the plan He designed to use me to help walk other women through the pain of losing a baby.

I pray that women in a similar position to me during the most difficult time of my life would find their way to scriptures that would lead them to heal, as I did. The Word is living, breathing, and active. The day I shut that Bible, God was telling me He had it all under His control and would use this to bring healing to others. I didn't see it at the time, but God's hand was upon me and leading me to the path of healing and kingdom purpose. It was up to me to choose the path. I wish I had chosen His path instead of my own a lot earlier. I did a lot of worldly living and looked for a savior in everybody but the true Savior, Jesus Christ. I heard a preacher talking about the woman at the well, as told in John 4:1–26. I saw myself in this woman, and like her, He drew me into a relationship with Him.

God never changed, but I did. Whoever left that Bible open knew I needed Him to lead me through the pain. It says in Hebrews 13:8, "Jesus Christ is the same yesterday, today, and forever." Jesus never stopped leading me, even when I chose my own path.

If we trust Him in all things, He will lead us in the way we should go.

Chapter Six

Something Old, Something New, Something Borrowed, Something Blue

"A time to weep, And a time to laugh; A time to mourn, And a time to dance" (Ecclesiastes 3:4).

This story was beautiful. A literal triumph over tragedy kind of story. A mother and a grandmother brought both their wedding dresses on a Transformation Tuesday to make one angel gown for their daughter/granddaughter for the following Friday. You see, her baby was on life support, and they were going to let this tiny angel go home on Friday. They wanted an angel gown made from the mother's and the grandmother's wedding dresses. They watched with tears in their eyes as we tore the dress apart and added both dresses to make this perfect little angel gown for her baby to meet Jesus.

The mother had not been able to cry yet. It all felt like a bad dream, and she was going to wake up soon. I had never met this lady or really didn't know much about her story or her daughter's, but she could feel my story. She moved through a crowd of ladies and put her arms around me and just sobbed. She said over and over, "You know how I feel." Later, as the day went by, I was able to share my story with her.

You see, God places the right people in the right place for just the right time. He used me as a vessel to help walk with this lady that I would never see again through one of the most difficult times of her life. I explained to her that He had chosen me to be a mother to an angel baby and what an honor it was to do the work for Jesus. I pray for God to continue to use me in this ministry as I walk through the valley of the shadow of death with these families. That the light of Jesus will shine so strong that they have complete healing. I pray they will not just see me but will also see the Savior in me.

Her sweet angel went home to be with Jesus that weekend wearing a beautiful angel gown made from her mother and her grandmother's wedding dresses. She will not go to Prom or get married on this earth, but she was dressed for the ball and to dance with Jesus for the first time on the streets of gold, which must have been amazing. I can only imagine that glorious day!

"Therefore you now have sorrow; but I will see you again and your heart will rejoice, and your joy no one will take from you" (John 16:22).

The next story was that of an elderly couple. We did not know her personally but to know her story is to know her. She mentioned that she and her husband were married at a very young age; therefore, they were able to enjoy a lengthy marriage. We learned her husband's favorite color was blue, they even had a blue car, so it was natural for her to have her mother make her wedding dress the same color blue.

When we received her wedding dress, her husband brought the dress to us and told us she was now in a nursing home because he was unable to care for her. Her time on this earth was growing shorter by the day as she was now very sick. This couple lost their first child at birth, so our ministry was very touching to her. When she heard of our ministry, she wanted to donate her beautiful blue wedding dress because she knew very soon she would be leaving this earthly vessel to go home to be reunited with our Lord and Savior, Jesus Christ. She said she was looking forward to the day she would see one of "His" angels coming home in an angel gown made from her beautiful blue wedding gown. What a beautiful picture of heaven and of Jesus.

We always create before and after photos of the wedding dress and the angel gowns. This dress was no different. But we printed off the picture and mailed it to her husband. He took the picture, framed it, and placed the picture by his wife's bed. She would pass away less than a week after receiving the picture, and we never heard from him again. We don't know the end of the story, but God does.

An interesting little fact about how this book has come to-gether to tell the story of Angels In Waiting 91:4 is that during prayer, I received the titles of the chapters, not really knowing what the contents of the chapters would be. I wrote the title of this chapter, "Something Old, Something New, Something Bor-rowed, Something Blue," having no idea what was going into this chapter. Like God so often does for me, He highlighted the stories that needed to be part of this chapter. Even while writing this chapter, I didn't really understand how it would fit with the title. But suddenly, God told me that the first story was about a newer wedding dress and an older wedding dress that was being borrowed for her daughter's angel gown. The last story was about the blue wedding dress. Thus, how the chapter came together under the chapter title, which was given to me months before writing the contents of this chapter.

This is another example of how God knows the end from the beginning. You see, this book is not being written out of my flesh and how I would tell the story of Angels In Waiting 91:4. The book of Isaiah says it this way;

> For My thoughts are not your thoughts, Nor are your ways My ways," says the Lord. "For as the heavens are higher than the earth, So are My ways higher than your ways, And My thoughts than your thoughts."

Isaiah 55:8–9

The beauty of serving the Lord is that we don't have to have it all together and have everything figured out. There's no faith in that at all. God wants us to trust Him. When we let go of control over our circumstances and allow Him to move, He will far exceed even our wildest imagination. The process of getting to the end, or the goal, will rarely (if ever) look the way we think it should look. But we never see the big picture the way God sees the big picture. It's like our life is part of a giant mosaic. Our life is just one little piece of the puzzle, but it's an integral part of completing the picture. The broken edges of our life fit the overall picture perfectly.

The key is letting go of the things we think we can't control and allowing God to do what only God can do!

"Now faith is the substance of things hoped for, the evidence of things not seen" (Hebrews 11:1).

So, what does faith mean to you? How do you get faith?

These are just two of the questions that can come up when we start a conversation about faith. Faith can be earned through persevering through trials, and faith can be lost, but faith is truly defined by Hebrews 11:1. Hebrews chapter 11 is known as the faith chapter. There are several examples of biblical heroes that exhibited faith.

The basic idea of the word faith in both the original Hebrew and the Greek languages conveys the idea of faith being directly connected with truth or something that is trustworthy. (This is just one of the meanings conveyed in these languages.) When we are exercising faith in anything, we are believing that the thing upon which we have faith is true. Faith is a strong conviction or belief in something.

Faith is being assured in our convictions that what we are placing our hope in is actively being worked on by the Lord, even though we cannot physically see it. Faith knows that no matter the situation in our lives or in someone else's life, the Lord is working in it.

In Ephesians chapter 6, we are reminded that we are to put on the shield of faith as part of the whole armor of God. We are exhorted to use the shield of faith to quench the fiery darts the evil one shoots at us every day. But our understanding of the word "faith" is critical to using the shield correctly. Shields in combat are used to intercept specific attacks. It was a warrior's primary mode of defense. The shield was active and in motion. Therefore, faith should be evident in our actions. Faith, in spiritual warfare, must be put into motion in order to be raised up in defense.

If you've ever watched a movie where there were ancient battle scenes using a shield, you would know that the shield was a primary weapon used mostly for protection but could also be used on the offensive. A Roman soldier, for example, understood the importance of the shield in protecting themselves as well as those on either side of them. If a shield went down in battle, it could compromise the entire company of warriors. A lost shield would essentially create a weak spot in the defense strategy. The same is true of the shield of faith. Not only does the shield of faith protect us as individuals, but it also protects those near us.

Your shield of faith is vital in your battle plan. There is a gaping hole on the battlefield when you are not holding up your shield. God has uniquely created you with strengths and talents that others are not equipped with. Your role in the battle is irreplaceable. You bring something unique and necessary to the battlefield to not only fight our enemy but also encourage others fighting alongside us. Our enemy is a liar and the father of all lies. He never misses an opportunity to poison your own self-image, destroy your confidence, and break your will when you seek to serve the Lord. He seeks to break you down so that you have no impact on the ultimate battle plan. If he can take you out of the battle, he can separate you from God. He will try to convince you that you have nothing to offer and that you are insignificant in the battle.

But when we are not effective in the battle, or we fail to accomplish our part in the bigger mission, someone close to us becomes vulnerable to attack. Our enemy will do whatever it takes, so you do not realize the potential that God has created you with; you are a fierce warrior when operating in our God-given destiny to take down strongholds and build up kingdoms. You have what it takes to be a mighty warrior in God's army! But you must put your faith into action to build strength in yourself and encourage others to do the same. Living out our faith can be: making church attendance and serving a priority, breaking addictions and generational curses, getting out of debt, staying sexually pure until marriage, offering forgiveness, etc.

It's your job to hold up your shield of faith for your children, grandchildren, and those you love and care about until they can hold up their own shield in the battle. A shield will not raise itself; it is useless without the strong grip of the warrior to lift the shield in protection. Once the shield is effectively implemented, it will extinguish every flaming arrow of the enemy. Take up your shield, warrior, and wield it effectively.

Guard yourself against losing your faith. For you become vulnerable, and those you love will be vulnerable too. Stand strong! When we can do nothing else, simply stand and do not be moved!

The Bible tells us to stand firm in the faith and be strong (1 Corinthians 16:13). It also tells us to stand firm in Philippians 4:1. Or how about being steadfast and immovable (1 Corinthians 15:58)? If you want more, go do a word study on "stand" in the Bible. I think you will be encouraged and inspired to take your stand for faith when you do.

Chapter Seven

Never Made It to the Altar

"For in the resurrection they neither marry nor are given in marriage, but are like angels of God in heaven" (Matthew 22:30).

She dreamed of marrying the man of her dreams, as she bought the most beautiful wedding dress ever, but God had other plans for her. You see all things flow through His hands; we just trust the process and follow Him. He is a good Father who is very faithful all the time, even in death. He is so worthy!

This mother was diagnosed with breast cancer and was not able to overcome the disease. She suffered for six years before succumbing to the brutality that is cancer. Another life cut far too short. She had prophetically purchased this wedding gown in hopes of wearing this wedding dress at her fairytale wedding. Unfortunately, her dream wedding never happened.

A gentleman, the son of this mother, got in touch with us through my son and wanted to donate his mother's wedding dress. She never got to wear the dress and walk down the aisle with her prince charming; instead, she walked into heaven to meet her bridegroom. The son and daughter prayed over their mother's wedding dress and had decided to have it made into little angel gowns for the infants who were born sleeping or went to heaven shortly after birth. One of the angel gowns was given back to the son as a keepsake from his mother. I pray the family got the healing they both needed through this tiny angel gown made from their mother's wedding dress. Their mother never got to wear this wedding dress, but another precious angel will get to wear it in heaven, and someday, she may see this tiny angel walk into heaven in the angel gown made from her very own wedding dress.

I met with this young man and gave him the angel gown made from his mother's wedding dress, and he held it so close to him. I prayed this would bring him so much healing in his life. He will not see his mother again on this earth, but someday when he arrives in heaven, she will meet him there and tell him how proud she is of him for donating her wedding dress and for clothing so many little angels in her memory! This mother never made it to the altar, but her memory will live on throughout eternity.

Altars are important places. For many people, an altar is a place where you get married or a place where you can be left at the altar waiting. Nonbelievers mostly think of an altar in these, or similar, terms. In every religious culture, an altar is of utmost importance. In ancient times, the altar was a place of sacrifice where people could honor God with their offerings. It was a prominent place in the Bible as "God's table," a sacred place for sacrifices and gifts offered up to God.

Today, an altar is a place of separation where we separate ourselves to God and separate from generational curses and traits. An altar is a place of prayer and consecration.

Family altars are altars raised up to pray for the family. Your family altar is raised specifically to pray for your own individual family and for the needs of other people around you as you feel led and directed by the Spirit of God. For a genuine child of God, a personal prayer altar is a must-have, and for every genuine Christian family that is serious about walking in the ways of God, gathering at the altar regularly is a must. Altars and what we do there have the power to shape and alter the destinies of families.

In the Hebrew culture, the family altar is a critical part of the journey to knowing God and knowing the Torah, the first five books of the Bible. No…I'm not Jewish, but I do want to know more about the Jewishness of my Savior. As a child of God, I have been grafted into the family of God and His people. Romans 11:19 says, "You will say then, 'Branches were broken off that I might be grafted in.'" As a Gentile, I have been grafted in.

Someone in the Protestant faith is likely to view this as an unnecessary religious tradition that is considered a religious activity. If you are using the altar in a routine, then you may be right if you think that way. But if you view the family altar as a place of contact where you can experience God in a very personal way, then praying at the altar will be a life-changing experience.

Prayer is vital to the Christian life, and we are called to pray for all. In fact, Paul exhorts us in 1 Timothy 2:1, saying "that supplications, prayers, intercessions, and giving of thanks be made for all men."

> And he says nothing that would indicate some people are exempt from doing so. All believers in Christ have the Holy Spirit who helps us communicate our

prayer requests (Romans 8:26–27). All believers are to be praying in the name of Jesus, which means that Jesus Christ is our Lord and Savior, that we trust in Him for everything, including His interceding with the Father for us in all things, and that we live and pray in accordance with God's will. Praying in Jesus' name does not mean merely adding "in Jesus' name" to a prayer. Rather, it means praying in submission to His will. As prayer warriors, we rejoice in all things and have a spirit of thankfulness for what God is doing in our lives and the lives of others, and our own spirits grow day by day as we come to realize the magnitude of our blessings. We know with certainty that God provided the breath we just took (Isaiah 42:5); that He has forgiven our past, present and future sins (1 John 2:12); that He loves us with an eternal love (Ephesians 2:4–7); and that we have a place in heaven with our Lord (1 Peter 1:3–5). Our hearts, then, are filled with joy and peace and overflow with love for God, and we want others to have this same love, joy and peace. Therefore, we work for them by praying.[1]

My husband currently has an altar under construction; it will be placed in our prayer room (aka…my closet) underneath my prayer board. We are placing the Hebrew phrase *B'ezerat HaShem*, which means "with God's help," on our altar. The ministry of Angels In Waiting 91:4 is the result of much prayer. Every ministry decision came about through prayer. Our family, too, considers prayer as a primary weapon against the evil one and the wickedness he produces. We do not consider prayer as our last resort but as the most effective way of fighting the spiritual warfare in our lives. My prayer closet is my war room; it is a consecrated space that is considered sacred to me. Many hours and many, many prayers have been lifted in this space, and many answers to prayer have been received in this space, as well. I have watched the hand of God move in that closet time and time again.

The mother at the beginning of this story is now worshipping our Lord and Savior, Jesus Christ, at the altar in heaven. The altar, if one really stops to think about it, is a place where new life begins. Whether it is the new Christian brother or sister surrendering their life to Jesus for the first time, becoming the "new man" or "new woman," leaving the old life behind in favor of the new life in Jesus Christ, or maybe it's a couple getting married at the altar dedicating their life to one another in a covenant relationship, thus becoming one flesh promising to honor God and each other. In some cases, funerals are held at or near the altar, passing from physical life into eternal life.

I pray your life begins at the altar too. One thing is certain; God will never leave you waiting at the altar. As it says in the second half of Hebrews 13:5, "For He Himself has said, 'I will never leave you nor forsake you.'"

Chapter Eight

'Til Death Do Us Part

"Until then, there are three things that remain: faith, hope, and love—yet love surpasses them all. So above all else, let love be the beautiful prize for which you run" (1 Corinthians 13:13, TPT).

The next two stories are examples of how life comes to us in many unexpected ways. Life is full of surprises…some happy surprises and, sometimes, surprises that we pray we never experience. Any way you look at it, life comes at you fast.

The first story was that of a young family. This lady found out about our ministry through her church. As the story was told to us, her husband had been badly injured in a car accident and lived only about a year before ultimately going home to the Lord. The lady came to us less than a year after her husband's death when she brought her wedding dress to us to be transformed into angel gowns. She also provided some of her late husband's neckties for us to use in the angel gowns.

This husband and father left behind his wife and a young daughter. He and his bride had been happily married for seven-

teen years at the time of his death. While extremely broken and
hurting over this unexpected loss, this young woman was thinking of others in need. She thought about keeping the wedding
dress for her daughter but decided not to burden her daughter
with deciding to wear her mom's wedding dress. Instead, Angels
In Waiting 91:4 made a handkerchief from her wedding dress
embroidered with the dad's initials for their daughter to carry
during her own wedding so she could feel like part of her daddy
is with her during this special day.

This young woman was able to overcome the death of her
husband and was able to move forward with God's help and
provision. She remarried a little over two years after her first
husband passed away. She married another strong Christian
man who had children of his own. While the enemy stole life
away from her husband and the man she thought she would be
married to forever, God took the loss and gave her more than
she could ask for. No, it doesn't lessen the loss of her husband.
But it did give her and her daughter a second chance at a loving
family.

This was not the life she thought she would have when she
first got married. But God will always take our tragedies and
turn them into triumphs if we simply trust the Father.

The second story was that of a lady that came to us through
friends she worked with in the NICU. She was familiar with
our ministry through her nurse friends. She decided she wanted
to be part of the ministry by donating her own wedding dress.
The ministry really touched her heart.

Unfortunately, this lady was hit by a car while walking in
her neighborhood. She was not able to overcome her injuries as
she was killed instantly from the impact. This accident occurred

less than a week after she donated her wedding dress to our ministry.

She had two daughters that were young adults that we contacted shortly after their mother's death. We told them what their mother had done by donating her wedding dress, and we asked them if there was something we could do to help bring them some peace. We made two ring bearer pillows with their mother's initials, one for each of the daughters to carry in their future weddings.

Both stories illustrate how quickly life can change. Let's face it; we are not even guaranteed the next breath we breathe. There are no guarantees in this life. Think through your own life and examine the times when you have had a sudden change that impacted your entire life. Life is one big, calculated risk. In the United States, we tend to take for granted that family will always be with us, that we'll always have a good job, that our marriage will be a happy and long one, that our children will be happy and healthy...I could go on and on. The point I am trying to make is that we cannot rely on the temporal things of this world. The one sure thing we have is the love of God. No matter what life may throw at you...God loves you! Even if you don't believe in Him or deny His power in your life, God still loves you. We may not recognize His love, or we may even think He hates us when we experience losses in our life. But the truth is no matter how mad you may get at Him or how much you deny Him, He still loves you and does not want you to be separated from Him.

The Word of God says in the book of Second Peter,

"The Lord is not slack concerning His promise, as some count slackness, but is longsuffering toward us, not willing that any should perish but that all should come to repentance" (2 Peter 3:9).

It is His desire that all be saved. Each and every one of us is a child of God. We may not all recognize that fact, but He ransomed each of us with the blood of His Son, Jesus Christ. We have been purchased at a price. Once we have a born-again experience, we belong to Jesus and are seated in Christ in heavenly places. Salvation is free, but it is not cheap!

So, if we place our faith and trust in Him and turn from our wicked ways, He is faithful and just to forgive us of all unrighteousness. Our name is written in the Book of Life. But we deny Him through our sin. We are called to repent of our sins. So, when life brings a drastic change in our natural life, He gives us the strength to withstand in the Spirit.

Remember, we come from dust, and to dust we shall return.

"In the sweat of your face, you shall eat bread Till you return to the ground, For out of it you were taken; For dust you are, And to dust you shall return" (Genesis 3:19).

As you can tell from the stories above, while our ministry is mostly about angel gowns, we also provide keepsakes for the families of these children born sleeping or go to Jesus shortly after birth. We have made custom handkerchiefs, ring bearer pillows, and have even provided angel gowns for shadow boxes for these families. This ministry is much more than just sewing gowns together. We also hope to walk these families through a difficult time of grief, and we can truly sympathize with their loss.

By providing these keepsakes, we are hoping to give these families a remembrance of their child or other family members and legitimize their loss. Their family member's life mattered.

Many people feel uncomfortable talking about the loss of a baby and/or their family members. But statistics show that one in four women will experience this loss. We want these families to know they are not alone. That is why we will gladly provide these keepsakes when asked.

Providing keepsakes is just one of many ideas that were given to us by God. My marriage is a source for some of the ideas we have come up with to make the ministry run. Our marriage is divinely ordained, and God put us together in a most unusual way and ultimately led us to run with God's plan for Angels In Waiting 91:4.

My husband, Todd, and I were married on a beach in South Georgia. Ours was a sudden love story. God led us to each other after some past difficulties. We both were broken in many ways. The places in each of us where we were individually broken were areas where the other was strong—like two broken hearts that fit together perfectly. Together we made a whole person. We were literally designed for each other. There was no period of adjustment or anything like that…ours is a marriage like a hand in a glove. At the center of it all, Jesus is there.

On that warm, sunny day on the beach, we said our vows to each other and meant every word for the first time in our lives. We were determined to have no other way out of our marriage, so we chose to leave the "D" word out of our vocabulary no matter what. I'm not saying we haven't had difficulties since we got married; Lord knows that we have had many storms. But God has been faithful to lead us on a path to solidarity with each other and a love that neither of us has ever had before.

Due to our broken pasts, we both were on a path to healing the wounds we had endured before we met. This was *huge*!

We both had finally surrendered to Christ and allowed Him
to have His way in us prior to meeting each other. Jesus is the
cornerstone of our marriage. Our lives are built upon Him, and
our marriage and devotion to one another are products of our
relationship with our Savior, individually and as a couple. That's
what I meant when we said those vows on the beach. We stood
there before God and witnesses attesting to our unified life built
upon Jesus Christ; every word spoken was vitally important. We
never knew then that our journey ahead would lead us into this
ministry. Ecclesiastes 4:12 comes to mind here; it says, "Though
one may be overpowered by another, two can withstand him.
And a threefold cord is not quickly broken." The cord of three
strands represents God, the groom, and the bride. Braiding
these three strands symbolizes the joining of one man, one
woman, and God in the marriage.

But God always has a bigger plan. The beginning of our
marriage was no different. We started off thinking we would
have this beautiful, happy life leading us into the rest of our
lives. We never anticipated the many twists and turns our life
together would take. We have experienced more in eleven years
of marriage than most marriages have experienced in a lifetime. The ministry of Angels In Waiting 91:4 was one of those
twists. A turn we never expected. God has taught us how to be
ministers of the gospel of Jesus Christ, how to love each other
and others, how to be stewards of the ministry He gave us, and
who to connect ourselves with. God has completely led the way
through much prayer and intercession in our marriage and our
ministry.

Our marriage is critical to making this ministry work as
well. Being one flesh, we are in a constant state of prayer and

intercession for Angels In Waiting 91:4. Not to mention all the behind-the-scenes work that goes into running a ministry. All the setup and tear down, the cleaning, the administrative work, the inventory tracking, etc. All of this is done by our family. We do, on occasion, get additional help from our volunteers, but mostly all of this is done by my husband, me, and one of our sons.

God has laid out many of the processes we use in the ministry, but He has given it to us to run with as we see fit. But again, we do nothing unless we receive confirmation through prayer and intercession. The monthly newsletter sent to sub-scribers, the blog, the book, and how we run the weekly Trans-formation Tuesdays are all divinely inspired. My husband and I, as a team, refine what God gives us to do, and we have devel-oped certain ways of operating that work for this ministry.

When one decides to start a ministry having the support and effort of those you love is vital to making it run smoothly. There cannot be conflict within the marriage over how a min-istry is established and run. It just won't work when conflict is present. As it says in Mark 3:25, "If a house is divided against itself, that house cannot stand." That does not mean that we have agreed on every little detail. But largely, we agree mostly on everything, but God always has the final say. We both take these disagreements to prayer and wait for His answer before moving forward. Fortunately, I am the big picture, type "A" per-sonality that drives the ship. While my husband is a detail-ori-ented person figuring out how to make things work efficiently.

Our marriage has been a match made in heaven in more ways than one!

A marriage is a covenant relationship before God and

others. A wedding, when done biblically, is a picture of the marriage supper of the Lamb. This is described in more detail in Revelation 19:7–10. Basically, Jesus Christ is the perfect Lamb of God that offered up His life as a substitute for ours. As the perfect Lamb of God, He is the bridegroom, and we, as the church, are His bride. One day we who are in Christ will sit with Him at the great wedding feast. Oh, what a glorious day that will be!

Chapter Nine

Double Portion

Instead of your shame you shall have double honor,
And instead of confusion they shall rejoice in their
portion. Therefore in their land they shall possess
double; Everlasting joy shall be theirs.

Isaiah 61:7

What's the story of this dress? A mother came to donate her grandmother's wedding dress for us to make into angel gowns. This young, beautiful woman knocked on the door. She was accompanied by her mother and her set of twins. We welcomed them in, and they started to share their story.

Why Angels In Waiting 91:4 and why now? She begins to explain this wedding dress was her grandmother's, and it had been worn by seven different women in their family, including her grandmother. Wow, seven different women wearing the same wedding gown! Imagine how the world of fashion had changed throughout the length of time that these seven family members had worn this dress. There was a simple elegance to this dress that withstood the test of time. This was such a beautiful story! But there was more...much more to this story.

She asked us if she could deliver the angel gowns with her grandmother that were made from this dress to the hospital for us. When we asked her which hospital and why this was so important to her, she explained to us that just three years earlier, she had lost a full-term baby and wanted to give these angel gowns in honor of her angel baby. With tears in her eyes, she shared that she carried her baby full term, and when she delivered her, the baby was born sleeping. With pain in her voice and tears in her eyes, she expressed how she struggled with the loss still, and she hoped that this would somehow help with the healing process.

She told us that this would allow her to be able to give back to the hospital, which held a special place in her heart. The loss of her baby was as fresh and real as it was the day her baby went to heaven three years ago. And now God has given her a set of healthy twins! She got a double portion for her pain. Nothing can take away the pain of the loss of her first sweet angel, but there is always a rainbow at the end of a storm.

In returning to their suffering, Israel received a double portion with everlasting joy. I think when we read the scripture in Isaiah 61:7 (the verse referenced at the beginning of this chapter), it's easy for us to skip over the last part of that verse. We want to concentrate on the double portion. Human nature always wants more than what we have. But can you imagine having everlasting joy? Even writing this now, I'm not sure I can comprehend the concept of everlasting joy. Stop what you're doing and think about that for a moment. Everlasting joy...what would change in your life if you had everlasting joy?

The second half of Nehemiah 8:10 says, "Do not sorrow, for the joy of the Lord is your strength." So, if you need more strength to endure or to be able to move on from your past or whatever, then seek the joy of the Lord. The joy of the Lord is where your strength comes from. Any other source of strength that is of the flesh will not endure. But the strength that comes from the Lord will last.

With more joy, everlasting joy comes more strength...an everlasting strength in Jesus Christ. His great love, His mercy, and His grace should be the ultimate source of joy for those of us who believe. What can be better than that? The gift Jesus has given us, salvation through the cross, is the greatest gift one could ever hope for...that while we were still sinners, Christ died for us (Romans 5:8). We get to experience eternity with Jesus and our loved ones who have paved the way ahead of us. They are waiting for us...can you imagine the welcoming party awaiting you when you get to heaven? All you must do is be born again and believe in Jesus Christ as your Savior, that He died for your sins. So why not repent of your sins now and accept Jesus as your Savior if you haven't done so already?

Several times in the Bible, specific reference is made to a "double portion." When someone receives a double portion, he gets a gift twice as much as that given to others.

The lady at the beginning of this chapter just happened to get two rainbow babies as her double portion. A rainbow baby is a baby born after a loss of a baby through stillborn, miscarriage, or an infant that dies soon after birth. They are called a rainbow baby because there is always a rainbow after a great storm, and let me tell you, losing your baby is a storm. When you leave that hospital without your baby, you feel the brokenness deep down inside. You feel like you will never heal from this pain, but I am here to tell you that, through Jesus Christ, there is healing. I have a son who is my rainbow baby; even though he is thirty-five years old now, with a daughter of his own, I still have such a connection with him. He is not loved more than the other boys, but I always look at him and see the rainbow at the end of the worst storm of my life. God sent this tiny little human that gave me hope and a promise that God is still God, and God is still good. To God be the glory!

The pregnancy after my first son's death was both exciting and very scary. I was afraid of the baby showers, every doctor appointment and follow-ups, and all the little details scared me to death. I was so afraid that I didn't even want to tell people I was pregnant again. My pregnancies were all very complicated and required a surgical procedure in the second trimester in order to be able to carry my babies to full-term. So up until this point, I was very nervous and filled with anxiety. I felt very alone with no one that I could talk to about this situation. Even though I was pregnant, this was a very dark time. Without the surgical procedures, I would not have been able to have any children. I was so very grateful to have a doctor with knowledge of what to do and how to handle my physical deficiencies. Without God leading this physician, I would not have had my other four sons.

I remember when the doctor held up my son for the first time, and he was alive and well; the flood of memories came rushing back about my son Brandon's birth and subsequent death. The enemy came in immediately to plant fear of losing my rainbow baby. But God came and replaced the fear and anguish with a downpour of His love and instantly placed an overwhelming love for my new son in my heart. It is important to note that my rainbow baby wasn't a substitute for my son, Brandon. It's a different kind of love altogether…an all-consuming love, much like our Father in heaven loves us. The Passion Translation says in Romans 5:8, "But Christ proved God's passionate love for us by dying in our place while we were still lost and ungodly!"

I now have received my double portion. My oldest son has not only been my rainbow baby, but he and his wife have also given me a precious granddaughter. Through it all, the pain of loss and the joy of new life, I have gained a great appreciation and deep, deep love for the Father who has blessed me with four sons after losing my first. My rainbow baby, my oldest son, didn't replace Brandon, but he is a reminder of God's great love for me and the blessings He has given me.

Chapter Ten

Heavenly Salute

After these things I looked, and behold, a door standing open in heaven. And the first voice which I heard
was like a trumpet speaking with me, saying, "Come
up here, and I will show you things which must take
place after this."

Revelation 4:1

I had to deliver a box of angel gowns to Duke University
Hospital in North Carolina. As I sat on the bench waiting for
the car to be pulled around to pick me up, I sat down next to
an older gentleman. He spoke rather softly and said, "Hello,
ma'am." I returned with a smile and said hello. He introduced
himself as Lonnie, and he was a retired military man. I thanked
him for his service, and he tipped his hat at me as if to say,
"You are welcome." He was such a humble man after Jesus' own
heart.

I was rather tired from the drive and the visit, so I wanted to just sit there quietly and listen to the birds and sounds
around me, but God had other plans. Lonnie began a conversa-

tion and started speaking life into me. Immediately, I knew this was a divine appointment from God. He asked me who I was in Christ? He told me many things, but the thing he really spoke loudly to me was the need to read the book of Revelation out loud, daily, until the Lord calls me home. He said, "The Lord is coming back, and I need to be prepared." I shook his hand as my car arrived for me to leave. I got into my car, and as I was driving away…the retired handicapped gentleman stood at the edge of the paved circle and saluted me. It was the most beautiful Holy Spirit-filled thing I'd ever been a part of. Tears rolled down my eyes as I passed him, standing at full attention as the vehicle passed by him.

This precious vessel that God had just used for His glory would forever be embedded in my heart. I was reminded of John 13:3–7, which says;

> Jesus, knowing that the Father had given all things into His hands, and that He had come from God and was going to God, rose from supper and laid aside His garments, took a towel and girded Himself. After that, He poured water into a basin and began to wash the disciples' feet, and to wipe them with the towel with which He was girded. Then He came to Simon Peter. And Peter said to Him, "Lord, are You washing my feet?" Jesus answered and said to him, "What I am doing you do not understand now, but you will know after this."

Jesus became a servant leader at this moment where He washed the feet of His disciples, becoming an example for us to follow. We must take notice of moments in time, such as my meeting with Lonnie, when He sends His messengers as servants to us. Lonnie was definitely a divine messenger for me. Was Lonnie an angel in disguise? I can't say for certain, but it sure did feel that way at the time I met him. More on this in a moment.

The tears of joy continued to pour down my face as I realized just what truly happened on that bench that day with Lonnie. Never underestimate what Jesus can do when you think it's going to be just a simple day. Always make room in your life for the Holy Spirit in any and all situations. Lonnie's name is written in my Bible with the date the Lord let me meet this precious soul. And as I read the book of Revelation, I pray and think of Lonnie, and I am thankful God allowed me to meet him and get his heavenly salute. I wonder, when I get to heaven, will Lonnie be standing there in his military uniform to salute me there?

One of our noblest moments that await us will come at the wedding feast of the Lamb. Our Lord will rise and begin to call forward all who were wounded in the battle for His name's sake, and you will be honored and your courage rewarded. Can you imagine that? Our precious heavenly Father coming toward you, with nothing but love in His eyes and saying, "Well done, good and faithful servant; you were faithful over a few things, I will make you ruler over many things. Enter into the joy of your lord" (Matthew 25:21).

Friends, can your heart and mind even comprehend that? What a glorious day that will be to see my sweet Savior face to face. To finally, be full in Christ and be made whole, as we were created to be! Hallelujah! Personally, I am looking forward to the day I will be made whole and in the image of Jesus. This world has nothing to offer me. I want Jesus. I pray as y'all read this book that it stirs something in you that makes you want more of Him, too.

Every now and again, we have supernatural encounters with the spirit world without even knowing it. I believe this was the case with Lonnie. The truth is, I think Lonnie might have been an angel in disguise sent to give me a message. Have you ever had an encounter where it just stuck with you...where you can remember every little detail? This meeting with Lonnie was amazing, and I can remember it like it was yesterday. While speaking with Lonnie, I had the feeling that I needed to make a special note of this time and pay special attention to every word. Lonnie was a soldier...a soldier in the Lord's army! I salute you, Lonnie!

Angels are spirit beings. They do not have a physical body like us, but they can appear in human form. In the Bible, when angels appeared to man, they appeared as natural men. I am reminded of the encounter Abraham had with two angels and the Lord Himself in Genesis 18:1–19. Abraham sat down and had dinner with these two angels and the Lord. This is the point where the Lord told Abraham that he would be the father of many nations. Abraham somehow knew this was a supernatural encounter even though they all appeared in the natural. So don't be quick to dismiss stories like that of Abraham and my own. You just might be entertaining angels in disguise.

"Do not forget to entertain strangers, for by so doing some have unwittingly entertained angels" (Hebrews 13:2).

Abraham's encounter with the heavenly beings created a vision for an entire nation, the nation of Israel. Whereas my encounter with Lonnie helped me to create the vision for Angels In Waiting 91:4.

Our vision statement reads:

"The Angels In Waiting 91:4's vision is to usher in divine healing of spiritual & emotional wounds that occur through infant loss due to a miscarriage, pregnancy loss, or through stillbirth."

The vision statement was created through much prayer and consulting with my mentor. This really comes back to my deepest pain. When my first son, Brandon, passed away at birth, the wounds that were created during this time were massive, and there was no one to offer any kind of counseling or comfort. The anger and pain of the loss were more than I could handle, and even the simplest of conversations would send me into a tailspin. Well-meaning people would try to help, but often the conversations did more to harm me than to heal my wounds.

So, the vision is to let the families who lose children know that there is hope and there is comfort in knowing that someone else has blazed a trail through the darkness. It makes the path to healing a little easier when you know you can walk in the steps somebody else has created. There is fear in the unknown for most people. There are many families that have endured the loss of a child; some have lost multiple children. If you can get to the point where you can share your pain with these families that have experienced the loss ahead of you, then you can build upon their stories to create your own. Just know this one simple truth; you are not alone.

People you haven't met yet depend on your story of healing. Therefore, we offer what we call Testimony Thursdays on our website and social media pages. These testimonies tell the stories of other families and how they have healed from their loss. As I said before, the pain doesn't really go away, but these stories can help you to identify with other families that have learned to cope with the loss in healthy ways.

There is hope after loss. Sometimes that hope lies in the afterlife. But there are definite requirements, the biggest of which is giving your life to Jesus Christ. Let's be clear about this, your motive for getting saved should never be to see your loved ones again and spend eternity with them. That is a major side benefit to being saved, however. But our priority should always be to spend eternity in heaven with our Savior, Jesus Christ. Once you are saved, you have the hope of spending eternity with your child in heaven. Your baby is anxiously awaiting your arrival. When your days on earth are done and you have finished the race, your child will welcome you home. But Jesus is our ultimate reward.

> He is the Bridegroom, and the bride belongs to him. I am the friend of the Bridegroom who stands nearby and listens with great joy to the Bridegroom's voice. Because of his words, my joy is complete and overflows!

John 3:29 (TPT)

I love how the Bible describes the ultimate hope of our days in heaven, as written in The Passion Translation in the book of Colossians.

Christ's resurrection is your resurrection too. This is why we are to yearn for all that is above, for that's where Christ sits enthroned at the place of all power, honor, and authority! Yes, feast on all the treasures of the heavenly realm and fill your thoughts with heavenly realities, and not with the distractions of the natural realm. Your crucifixion with Christ has severed the tie to this life, and now your true life is hidden away in God in Christ.

Colossians 3:1–3

And in the book of John, Jesus clearly says He has gone on ahead of us to prepare our home in heaven. All simply because you believe in the reality that Jesus Christ is our Savior and our salvation. He has redeemed us from the curse of the law.

In My Father's house are many mansions; if it were not so, I would have told you. I go to prepare a place for you. And if I go and prepare a place for you, I will come again and receive you to Myself; that where I am, there you may be also.

John 14:2–3

If all this is true, and the Bible is nothing but the absolute truth, then we cannot even imagine what is in store for us when we take our final breath on this earth and our first breath in heaven. What a glorious day that will be? Eternity in the most perfect place with no tears, with no heartaches, with no death, is truly heaven. And it's all available for you. I hope and pray to see you there one day!

"The Lord bless you and keep you; The Lord make His face shine upon you, And be gracious to you; The Lord lift up His countenance upon you, And give you peace" (Numbers 6:24–26).

Epilogue

I pray this book will help each of you reading it to heal
from your loss and get closer to Jesus. To seek His face and find
your purpose in His kingdom on earth until He calls you home.

There is hope. Another child does not replace the child that
was lost. When we have Jesus, it is not the end but only the
beginning. We hope and pray that if you, by chance, picked up
this book because of the title or the storyline or for whatever
reason, you understand this was a God-ordained moment where
God can start the healing process.

Jesus is here with blood-stained hands awaiting your surrender. Your child ran to those hands with such joy on their faces,
won't you do the same? Run, just run into the arms of Jesus and
allow Him to comfort you. He truly is the only way for you to
find peace in this lifetime. He is willing and able to heal you of
your brokenness.

For some of you reading this book, most of you really, it's
not just the loss of your child that needs healing. It might be
a prodigal child that has turned away from Christ. It might
be childhood wounds that have been untouched for decades.
It might be words that were spoken over you by people who

never really knew you. Whatever the case may be, God is telling you now, "Come to Me! I love you, and I have always been by your side, awaiting you to return to Me. Come home and let Me show you where your name is written in the Book of Life. I have written a book about your life; let's complete the work together; there are chapters left to be written. But I need you to surrender your life completely to Me. I need you to let Me love you the way I want to love you. I have much to show you, and someday I will answer all your questions. But for now...I need you to trust Me."

I leave you with the words of Jesus Christ Himself:

I leave the gift of peace with you—my peace. Not the kind of fragile peace given by the world, but my perfect peace. Don't yield to fear or be troubled in your hearts—instead, be courageous!

John 14:27 (TPT)

Shalom!

About the Author

Jean is a faithful follower of Jesus Christ with an extreme love of Scripture and the study thereof. She is a devoted wife, mother to five wonderful sons, three angel babies with several daughters-in-law, and a Mawmaw to six beautiful and much-loved grandchildren and two boxers named Malachi and Queen Esther.

She has devoted her life obediently to the call of God to start and run Angels In Waiting 91:4 non-profit ministry. She gives all the glory to her heavenly Father, Jesus Christ! Her desire is for this ministry to be nameless and faceless.

- Please visit www.angelsinwaiting914.com to learn more about the ministry.
- Her background is in dentistry, which was her passion for many years prior to starting Angels In Waiting 91:4.
- Jean lives in Braselton, Georgia, with her husband and most of her family around her.
- She is an active part of a local church and attends KINEO Ministry Training Center for further education.

In Jean's own words, hear how she describes herself:

I am the daughter of the King, Most High, and I will *not* be shaken!

I am His!

I was born for such a time as this! I am a modern-day Esther. I was born to be used by God Almighty to save my entire family! The Lord is training and preparing me for the coming days. My calling is unique, so my preparation much also be unique. He has called me out of darkness to be light to His world. The fullness of His power is coming upon me. I am living in the shadows of His glory. He is calling me to a place of influence to touch many lives. I am an empty vessel asking God to use me. "Also I heard the voice of the Lord, saying: 'Whom shall I send, And who will go for Us?' Then I said, 'Here am I! Send me'" (Isaiah 6:8).

God will shine through who I am becoming. I am resting in the love of my Father because I am who He says I am!

Endnotes

1   "How Can I Become a Prayer Warrior?" GotQuestions.org, February 26, 2011. https://www.gotquestions.org/prayer-warrior.html.

CPSIA information can be obtained
at www.ICGtesting.com
Printed in the USA
BVHW032301270922
648083BV00014BA/1407